RELAXATION & MEDITATION

EFFORTLESS

FLOWER COLORING BOOK

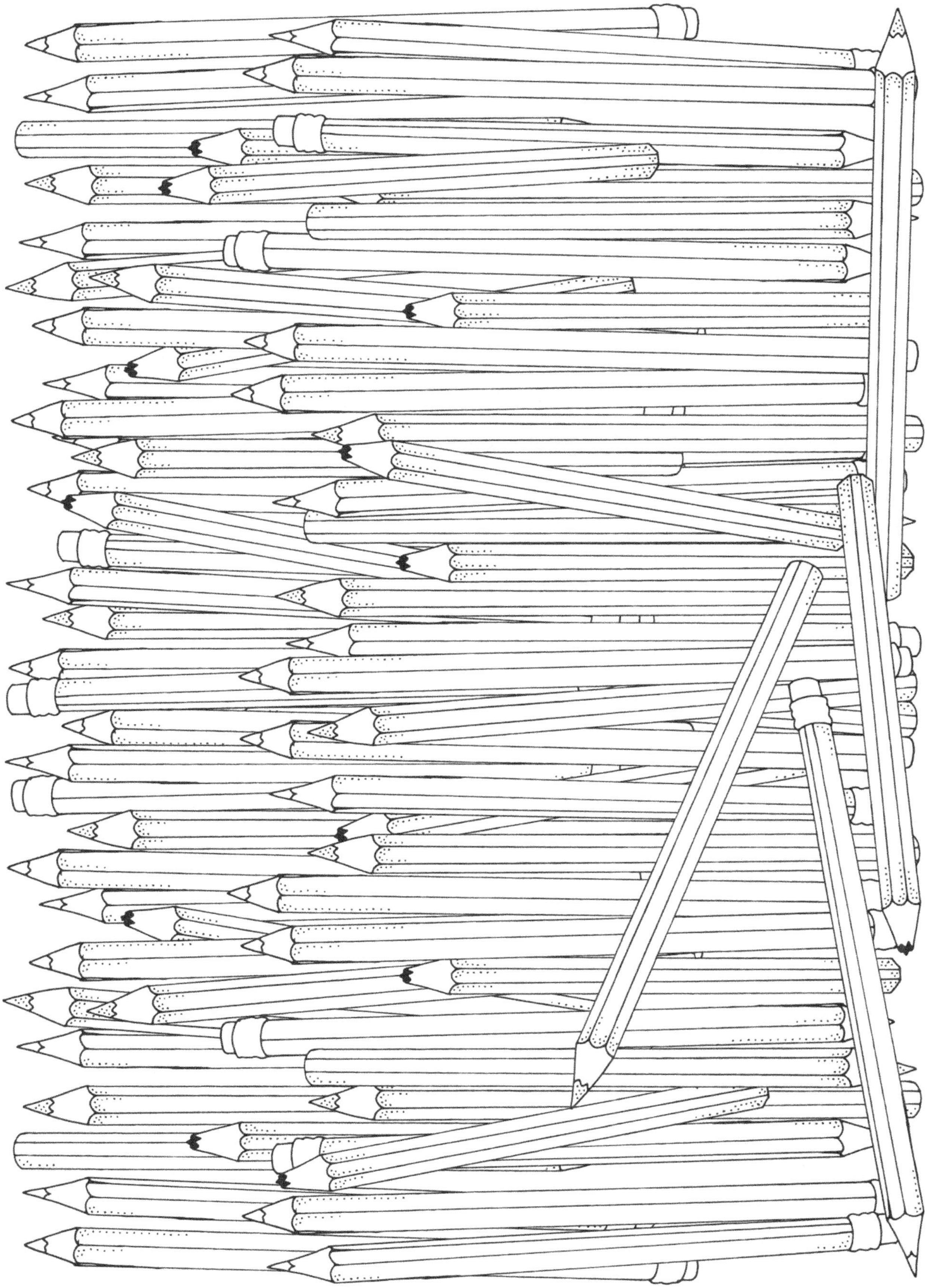

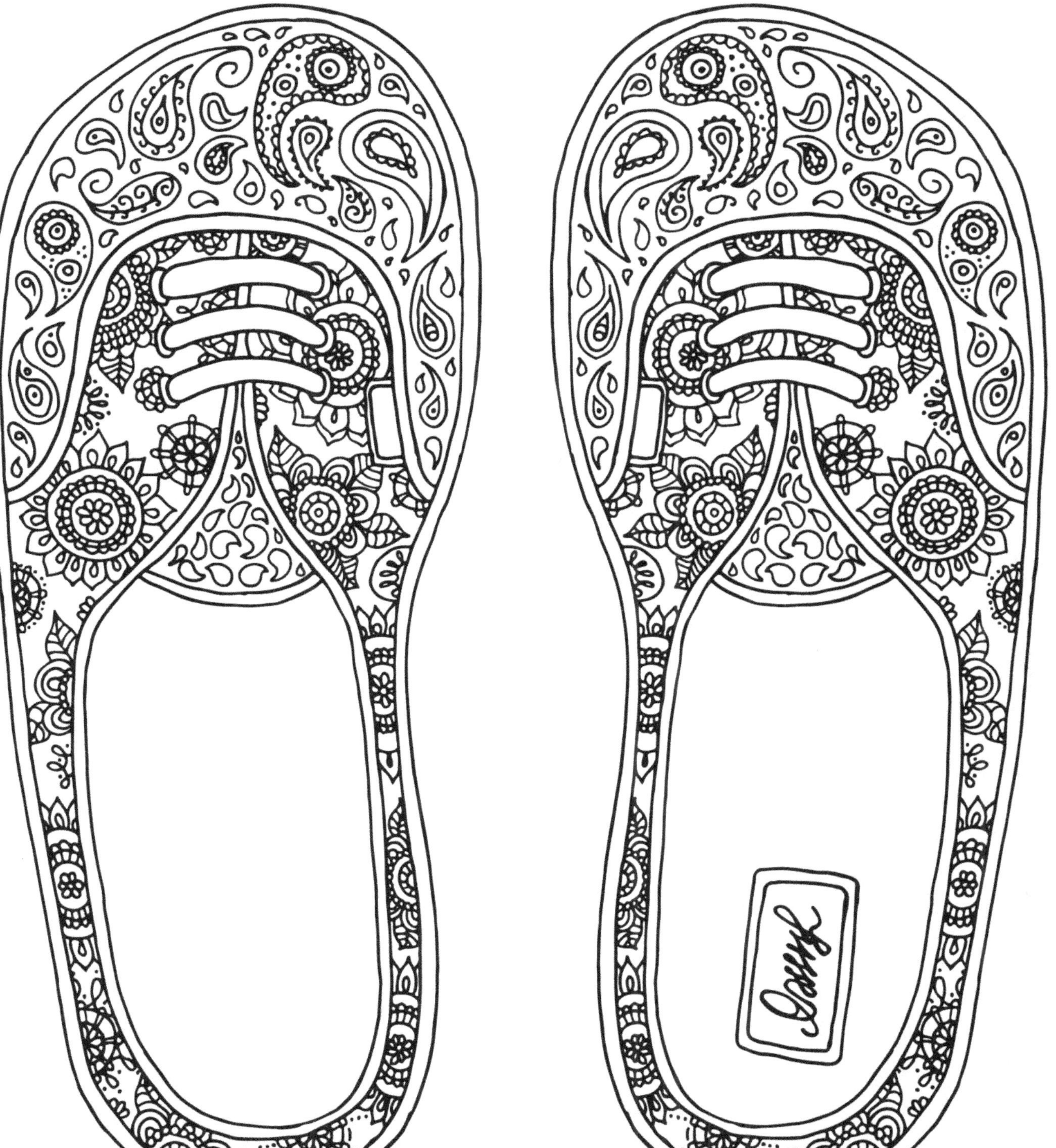

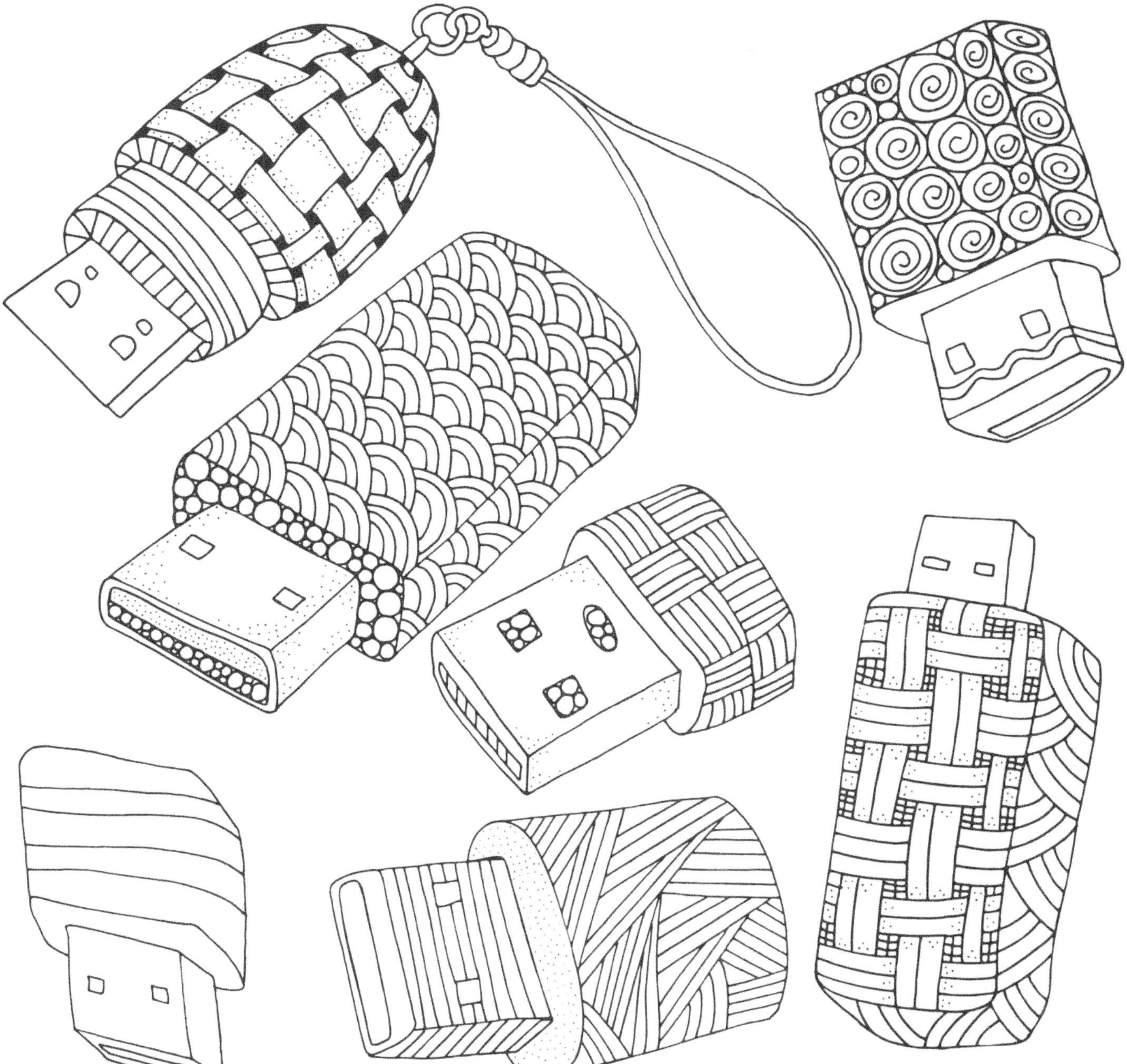

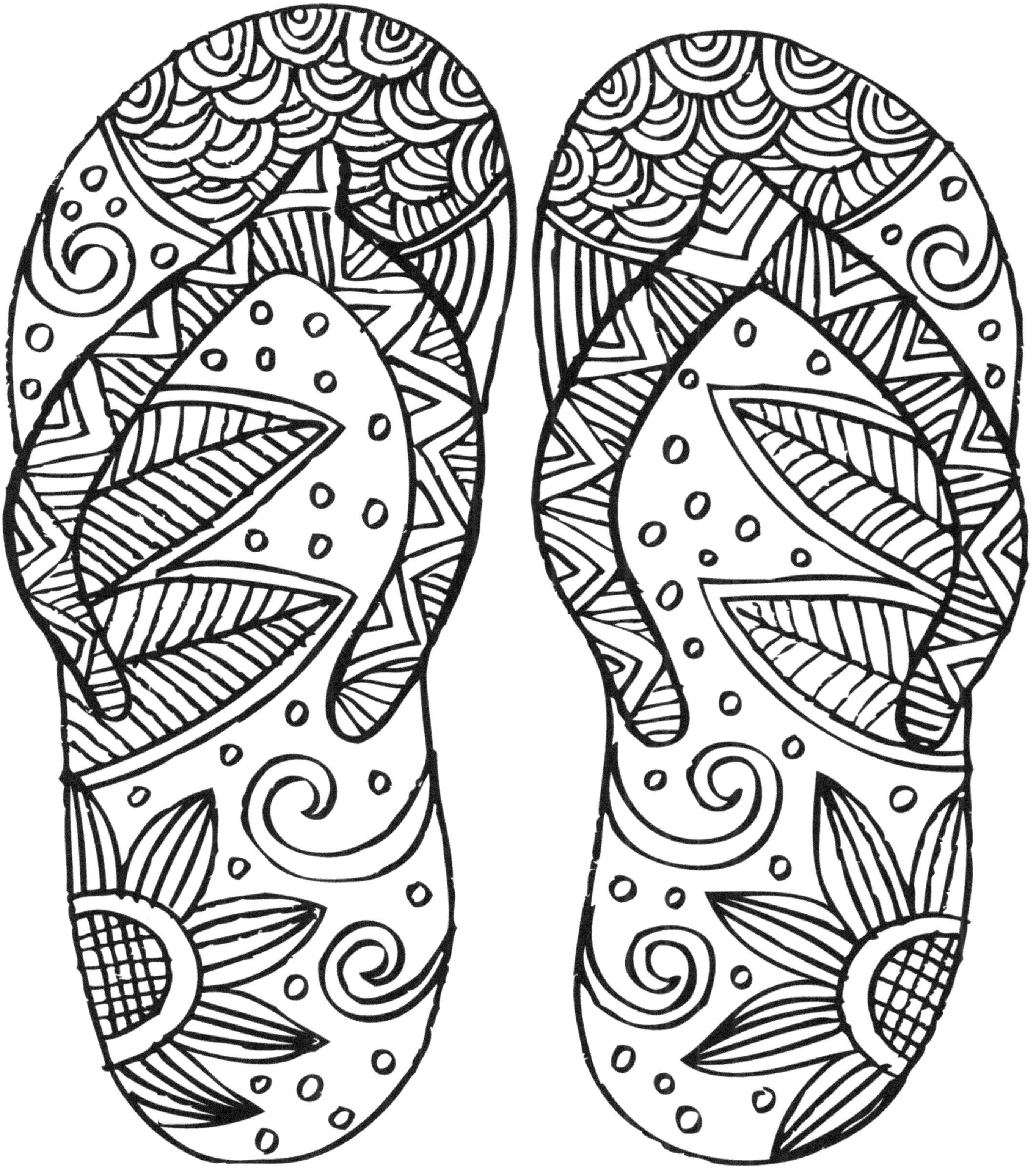

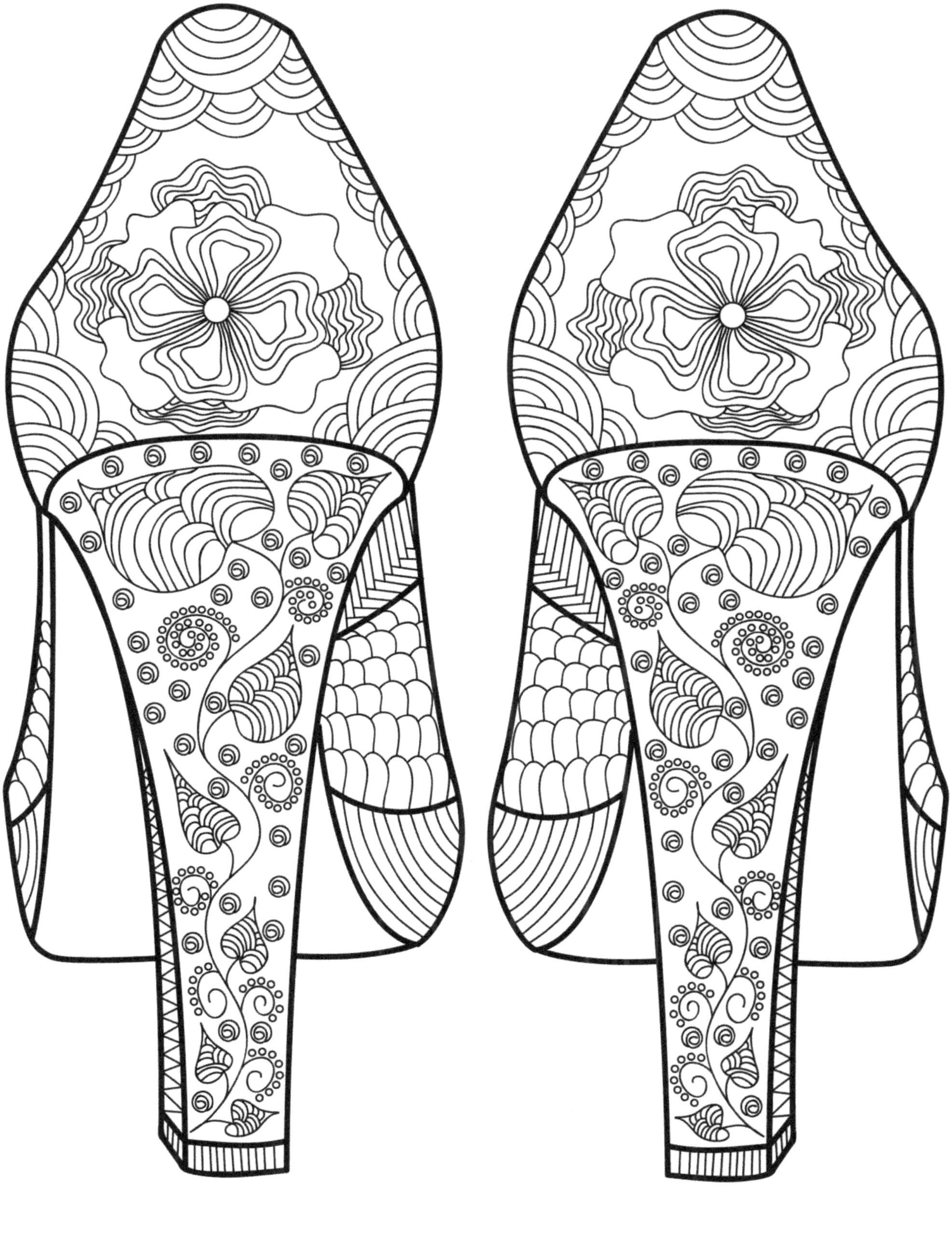

www.ingramcontent.com/pod-product-compliance
Lightning Source LLC
Chambersburg PA
CBHW081154280526
45787CB00008B/3328
* 9 7 8 1 5 4 8 3 2 0 3 6 2 *